1 MONTH OF
FREE
READING

at

www.ForgottenBooks.com

By purchasing this book you are eligible for one month membership to ForgottenBooks.com, giving you unlimited access to our entire collection of over 1,000,000 titles via our web site and mobile apps.

To claim your free month visit:

www.forgottenbooks.com/free475015

ISBN 978-0-483-84455-1
PIBN 10475015

CARNEGIE DUNFERMLINE TRUST.

SPECIAL REPORT OF

Conference of Gymnastic Teachers

AND

Organisers of Physical Training,

HELD IN THE

Carnegie Dunfermline Trust College of Hygiene,

On April 29 and 30, and May 1 and 2, 1907.

DUNFERMLINE:

PREFATORY NOTE.

THE attention of the Carnegie Dunfermline Trustees having been drawn to the need of co-ordination in the teaching of physical training in the schools of Scotland, it was decided to hold a Conference on the subject in the Dunfermline College of Hygiene, at which teachers of physical training, inspectors, and others interested might have an opportunity of exchanging views. There was a very gratifying attendance, teachers from all parts of the country being present and taking part in the discussions. At the close of the meetings, a general desire was expressed that a report of the proceedings should be published for circulation. The Trustees very willingly agreed to do so, and they trust that the report which is now issued will be found helpful in promoting the interests of physical culture. They desire to express their gratitude to Mr Scougal, and other inspectors, who favoured them with their presence, as well as to the teachers and others interested who took part in the discussions. A course of eight lectures on "The Physical Development of the Child," delivered by Miss Alice Ravenhill during the Conference, added greatly to its interest and usefulness.

CONTENTS.

FIRST DAY'S PROCEEDINGS.

"THE AIMS OF THE HEALTH COURSE,"

By Miss L. M. RENDEL,

Of the Carnegie Trust College of Hygiene and Physical Training.

Sheriff SHENNAN Presiding.

THE CHAIRMAN expressed pleasure at the presence of so many representatives from other parts of Scotland, and extended to the visitors a cordial welcome on behalf of the Carnegie Trustees.

MISS RENDEL delivered a lecture on "The Aims of the Health Course." She described the objects of a continuation course of domestic economy and physical training for girls which she started last autumn. She had been struck with the number of girls of the upper working classes and of small shopkeepers who, although they left school as soon as they were fourteen, did nothing for weeks, sometimes months, but "help" at home in a very perfunctory manner until some post in shop or factory turned up. In many cases the situation was accepted regardless of their suitability for it, or as to whether it was a good opening for their future. Most girls were really quite unfit either morally or physically to begin work when they left the primary school. They were of an age when they were extraordinarily susceptible to all moral and social influences, and to let those influences be those of the workshop or factory, where a working girl necessarily spent the larger portion of her time, was, to say the least of it, a somewhat unsatisfactory experiment, and not one likely to help her to become the type of woman we so badly needed to-day in Scotland. From the physical point of view, also, it was not wise that girls of this age should work for long hours on end. The question arose as to what could be done to give these girls a good start in life.

It was, she felt, both useless and impossible under the present social conditions to start any large, expensive, or elaborate scheme; what was wanted was some form of instruction which, while giving the girls a training which would be useful to them in after life, would at the same time have as its chief aim their moral and physical welfare. She wanted it also to be a stepping stone between the rigid discipline of primary school life and the almost complete independence of a working girl's existence. She wished physical training—in the sense that " physical training is the right understanding and right application of all physical conditions necessary to healthy life "—to be the basis of her scheme, but she also realised that that was insufficient, and she came to the conclusion that the subjects which would fit in and help to bring about the results she desired were the various branches of domestic science. The physical training she decided to have taught consisted of Swedish gymnastics, games, swimming, and dancing, and the domestic economy subjects consisted of cooking, laundry-work, and dressmaking. Although many of the girls might not need the latter subjects until they had houses of their own, yet she felt that at that age, perhaps more than at any other, did Sir Phillip Sidney's remark hold good— "Each excellent thing once learnt serves as a measure for all other knowledge." In addition to this curriculum, she decided that very elementary lessons should be given in physiology and hygiene, and determined that the latter should be taught in the only possible way to girls of this age, namely, practically. Arrangements were also made for lectures on home-nursing, and a weekly lesson in English— chiefly with a view to making the pupils write a good letter, encouraging and advising them as to reading, etc. All the girls were medically examined, and their height, weight, and general development recorded.

The course extended over the four autumn months from October to January. The fee was fixed at 10s, and the girls were expected to get a simple outfit, which cost about 15s. She issued very simple prospectuses to the parents of girls who she knew had left or were leaving school, and before long she had twelve girls between the ages of fourteen and seventeen. At the end of the course in January eight of the twelve asked to be allowed to stay on for other four months, and, as only three new girls came forward, she decided to allow them to do so. The girls worked, as a rule, in the forenoon only. They had four gymnastic lessons weekly, a dancing and a swimming lesson, and some played hockey on Saturday mornings. They had one cooking lesson, lasting four hours, four hours dressmaking, and two hours laundry work a week. Two hours were devoted to hygiene and home nursing, and one hour to English.

Not the least important part of the instruction was the practical hygienic conditions under which the pupils were obliged to live. She had also tried to encourage reading along the right lines, and to create an interest in all matters of public importance. The girls she had had this winter had, on the whole, very much improved both in physique and, she thought, in general intelligence. They had most of them formed some idea at least of what they wished to work at in the future; and they had thoroughly enjoyed the whole session. If she had remained in Dunfermline, while making many minor alterations, she would have endeavoured to keep the same ends in view—namely, not to establish an elaborate piece of machinery which depended for its existence on rules, regulations, and red-tape, but to keep it as far as possible a simple but expanding scheme in which individual judgment could be used and individual licenses granted. Her reason for limiting the class to fifteen, or at most twenty, was that she did not want to form so large a community that it was necessary

for the sake of order and discipline to have endless rules
to which every girl of whatever temperament was obliged
rigidly to conform. For girls of the less educated classes,
whose home training at the best was very imperfect, it
seemed very necessary to give them as far as possible individual help and attention, in order to teach them to think
and act for themselves in the most rational way—a thing
in which she found them lacking. In dealing with small
numbers it was quite possible to maintain a good tone and
good work, and at the same time to grant many licenses,
to make many exceptions, and to treat each girl on her own
merits. She had tried to know the girls intimately, and
had also tried to discover for what work each was fitted,
and she would see that they were all given opportunities
of starting on the right lines.

In a town so richly endowed as Dunfermline such a
scheme was possible. She was not competent to judge
whether it was feasible elsewhere, although she thought a
somewhat similar course might be attempted where there
was a cookery centre and also a fully qualified Swedish
gymnastic teacher. She was most anxious to impress upon
her hearers that such a scheme might easily degenerate
into a mere lifeless organisation, and if that were the case
all they had left would be a somewhat inferior domestic
economy school for girls run on a small scale without the
advantages of the large ones to be found in the big towns,
and with all their disadvantages. She hoped she had
succeeded in pointing out that this continuation course for

girls had as one of its aims, not only the teaching of so much dressmaking, not only the improvement of physique, but also the training of character and the creating of ideals which would help girls to lead wholesome and rational lives, and to become useful women and good citizens.

DISCUSSION.

Miss RAVENHILL asked to what extent Miss Rendel exercised her personal influence over the girls?

Miss RENDEL—The actual time spent in teaching was about an hour and a half per day, but I devoted a great portion of my time to them otherwise—in going walks with them, or in reading with them.

Miss RAVENHILL—You spoke in your lecture about the afternoons being free, but I now gather from your reply that the girls spent the afternoons a good deal with you?

Miss RENDEL—I found that while the girls were nominally with their parents in the afternoons there was not much for them to do, and if I had continued the course I should have arranged definitely for afternoon work.

Miss ROBERTS—Perhaps it should be explained that the common room has been open to the girls during the afternoon.

Miss RENDEL—Yes, I arranged that the common room should be open to the girls for two hours every day, so that they might prepare their studies or do needlework under good conditions as to air.

Miss AINSLEY, Edinburgh, asked if Miss Rendel did not feel that it was difficult to make a permanent impression on girls of fourteen years of age, and that the course might have been more beneficial if the girls had been two years older?

Miss RENDEL—As a matter of fact some of the girls were fifteen or sixteen years of age. The younger girls were those on whom I created the least impression.

Miss AINSLEY asked if Miss Rendel considered that an hour a week devoted to English was in any sense adequate?

Miss RENDEL—I should try to devote more time to English, but I did not wish to frighten the girls by making them think they were continuing at school. The English lesson was chiefly designed to prevent their reading unwholesome literature. I do not think I endeavoured to get beyond novel reading, but the novel reading I recommended was of a good description. I encouraged them to talk on what they had been reading, and at the end of the session I am going to set a general knowledge paper.

Captain FOSTER asked if any physical defects had been discovered and attended to?

Miss RENDEL—Yes, two cases were treated at the College.

Mrs LESLIE M'KENZIE, Edinburgh, said that girls at school were taught cookery with very fine equipment, and she wondered if they were being trained for the positions they would ultimately occupy. She questioned whether one in a dozen girls would again see a gas stove, steam cooker, or thermometer. They would go home to a very small fire—in many cases a couple of ribs between two bricks, and a few cinders. It seemed to her that the girls were not being exactly trained for what they were going to be eventually, and she wondered whether, from their point of view, they should not get the home made the training ground. She was afraid they would require to begin with the mother, to teach her to train her girl, because it would be a place very like her mother's that she would ultimately land in.

Miss RENDEL said she had seen the homes of eight members of her class, and knew all the parents. The kind of girl she had was of a better class than the type of which Mrs M'Kenzie spoke.

Miss ROBERTS thought it would interest the visitors to know that Miss Rendel had spent a good deal of time in teaching the girls hygienic habits, and that at the beginning of the session she provided the members with tooth-brushes, etc., etc.

Mrs M'KENZIE said it was extremely gratifying to hear of this practical work. The true basis of hygienic teaching in elementary schools was the actual doing of things. She did not see that it did any good to lecture school children on anatomy and physiology. More benefit would result from insisting on personal cleanliness.

Miss RAVENHILL said that the results of practical hygiene were most remarkable in Denmark and Sweden.

The children were spotlessly clean in person and clothing. In Copenhagen the effect of school baths and physical training, on the formation of character, had far exceeded anything dreamt of. She was in touch with many of the headmistresses of infant schools who had started tooth-brush drill.

SECOND DAY'S PROCEEDINGS.

"THE REGULATIONS FOR TRAINING OF

SCOTTISH TEACHERS,"

By A. E. SCOUGAL, Esq.,

H.M. Senior Chief Inspector of Schools.

Dr ROSS Presiding.

MR SCOUGAL, who was announced to give "A Lecture of Definitions," said:—The special purpose of my talk—for it is only a quite informal talk that I have undertaken to give—is that of conference with the students of this College and some visitor teachers, with a view to enlightening them as far as I can upon the details of what is now required, under our regulations in Scotland for the training of teachers, in connection with the subject of physical instruction, to which they are devoting themselves. I shall make no general pronouncement upon this subject. I do not need to claim your interest in it; the fact that we are here shows we have the subject at heart, and I need

B

not dwell upon merely general considerations. But, before proceeding to the special points that I intend to deal with, it may be as well to make a few observations by way of introduction. I want to base anything I have to say upon this fundamental point, that we have come, Departmentally and as a country, to look upon physical training as an essential part of the education of the child— as much in its own way a part of the child's training during his school period as his mental or intellectual education. Then I want to say to those here who are acting teachers that I hope we have got rid of the idea that this is another new "extra subject," plastered on to what is very commonly called an overloaded curriculum. It is nothing of the sort. We ought to deal, in our educational problem, with *the child*—individualising, that is, the child as much as possible in the circumstances in which we have to work; and I claim that this physical training is just an essential part of our duty to the child—the development of that child *in every possible direction* during the time we take charge of it. It follows from the claims I have made that, in my own personal opinion, this subject is—to use the terminology of our official regulations—one of the "primary school subjects" which every trained teacher ought to be acquainted with, and have training in the teaching of. One other point I should like to make, and that is to emphasise the fact that; although we have had something that we called physical exercises (previously known by the unfortunate name of drill) in our schools, we look at the

matter now from a new point of view. We are not striving
to set up a system of adaptation of the military drill for
adults as part of our school work and school curriculum.
We face the problem now from the point of view of what we
can do for the training and development of the individual
child, intellectually, physically, and morally. Our point of
view is not that of the military instructor. It is that of
the kindly educator—might I say, collective parent?—
interested in all that concerns the hygienic welfare of the
child.

I think I may come now to more specific details. I am
told that a good many of you ladies come from England;
that you are not familiar with the technicalities of our
Scottish system; and that it is hoped I may be able to
give you some light on this matter, in special view of the
fact that, as I trust may be the case, a good many of you
may become teachers in our Scottish schools.

Turning to the new *Regulations*, let us go back to a
stage before that of the " junior student "—I mean that of
the ordinary pupil in school. Now, I hope that when our
system is thoroughly developed, every scholar in our
schools will get, during his school period, physical training
adapted to his stage of life and advancement and to
his own individual needs and conditions. The period of
primary school life will take the child from the age of
five up to the age of fourteen. The phrase " intending
junior students," in the Regulations, refers to senior
scholars from twelve to fifteen who may be looking forward

to becoming junior students. This last term is a special designation for scholars at the next higher stage who are looking forward to becoming teachers. These junior students are practically scholars in our higher grade and secondary schools for the three years from fifteen to eighteen. They have gone through the early school period and have received physical training then. They have also gone through the period of the intending junior student—the course of three years' instruction in our higher grade schools—between the years of twelve and fifteen, where again, I hope, they have been getting the benefit of systematic, properly adapted, physical training. Then we come to the junior student stage proper, when the scholars I am speaking of attend certain selected higher schools called Junior Student Centres, sent there on their own request and in the expectation that they will become teachers, but without a binding obligation of any kind.

In the Scotch Education Department's "Regulations for the Preliminary Education, Training, and Certification of Teachers for Various Grades of Schools," it is laid down in Article 8 that the curriculum to be approved by the Department must provide for the instruction of junior students in the following subjects:—"English; at least one language other than English; History; Geography; Mathematics (including Arithmetic) and Experimental Science; Drawing, and some form of Manual work (in case of girls. Needlework); Physical Exercises; Music." Here the point I want to make is, that specific training in physical exercises is made an indispensable part of the curriculum for these junior students. Physical training is *expected* in all schools, of course; but there is no doubt that, as far as junior students are concerned, and as far as schools which are recognised as centres for junior students are concerned, the Department will *insist* on proper provision for this physical training, and upon adequate staff and equipment for the carrying of it on. I would also call attention to Article 11 of the Regulations, which states that ".Managers shall submit for approval, as an integral part of the curriculum, a scheme for the systematic training of the junior students in the art of teaching each of the primary school subjects." I think Captain Foster is with me in this idea—that it is exceedingly desirable, and would be beneficial, that junior students who are looking forward to becoming teachers should, after they have gone through so many years of individual practice and training in physical exercises, have their minds directed towards the meaning of these exercises from the point of view of the teacher, and possibly should have some little practice in giving instruction in them to young children.

Then we come to the next stage, when these junior students have completed their curriculum as such and become what we call "students in full training"—that is, practically what we know at present as Training College students. With regard to students in full training, the requirements in the Regulations are:—"Article 22—For purposes of professional training the curriculum shall include instruction in the elements of School and Personal Hygiene, Psychology, Ethics, and Logic, and also in the principles of education, and in the history of educational systems and theories. It shall further provide for discussion of the methods of teaching each of the subjects of the Primary School curriculum, and for correlated practice under proper supervision.''

I may say that the view I have expressed as to physical training being an essential primary school subject was confirmed quite recently by a pronouncement of the Department in which they approved very heartily of the resolution of the Edinburgh Provincial Committee that instruction in physical training should be made part of the compulsory curriculum of every student, in connection with training in hygiene.

Let us now turn to Article 36, which has reference to the certification of teachers for what we call the General Certificate. This Article says:—'' The following special regulations shall obtain with respect to singing, drawing, woodwork, physical exercises, and, in the case of girls, needlework:—(a) Applicants for general certificates must have undergone a sufficient discipline therein during their course as students, or during any school course or courses accepted in lieu thereof. But the relative mark of proficiency shall not be essential to recognition as a certificated teacher.'' That, I should like to point out, is a rather important distinction. Physical exercises are to form part of the training of the certificated teacher, but they are looked upon as possibly one of the subjects in which the teacher may not, from personal characteristics, reach such a satisfactory level of acquirement either in the acquisition or in the teaching of the subject as to entitle him or her to a mark on the certificate that is issued. I think it quite justifiable that the loss of this mark should not be a bar to recognition as a certificated teacher. Whatever claims one may make for the importance of the subjects mentioned, I think we should all feel it would be a hardship if a teacher, otherwise perfectly qualified, should be rejected for the General Certificate through not coming up to requirements in one or other of these subjects. There is, however, another regulation in the second part of the Article which may be of special interest to those of you who are looking forward to teaching. This second regulation reads as follows:—"(b) In so far, however, as the subjects in question may, either now or at any future time, be compulsory in primary schools, no staff will, in normal circumstances, be held sufficient which does not contain an adequate proportion of teachers whose qualifications to teach the compulsory subject (or subjects) are attested, either by satisfactory marks of proficiency recorded on general certificates, or by special certificates issued in terms of Articles 47 and 48." These articles have reference to a class of teacher of whom we have not very many now; but a class for which, I hope, we shall get many valuable recruits from this College. I wish we had the same outlook in regard to male instructors.

These Articles 47 and 48 refer to "teachers of special subjects"—that is to say, teachers who do not hold the qualification for the ordinary work of a school, but who wish to devote themselves to special work—for instance, physical training. Article 47 is in the following terms:— "Persons who at the date of these Regulations may be actually serving as recognised teachers of certain special subjects will at once take rank as recognised teachers of these subjects in terms of this article. But except with regard to such persons, the Department may at any time require, as a condition of recognition, that any or every such teacher shall produce evidence of having been properly trained, with particular reference to the subject he is to teach." The essential point, and the whole aim of the Regulations, is to ensure that every teacher who teaches anything shall be properly trained with reference to his or her subject. We all know how very imperfectly trained, or not trained at all, a great many of our teachers of special subjects have been. The Article continues:—" Special certificates of qualification as teachers of these subjects will be granted by the Department to the holders of diplomas recognised by the Department for the purpose." One of the diplomas to be recognised is that of a Physical Training College—" for a special qualification to conduct physical exercises and school gymnastics." The Department makes the proviso "that the holder of the diploma has in each case reached a certain standard of general education, satisfactory to the Department, before entering upon his diploma course, and has successfully completed such part of the general course of professional training for teachers (Articles 19 and 22) as may be prescribed."

Now, I have done my best to interpret the Regulations so far as they apply to physical training. I have spoken about the ordinary school, the period of junior students, the period of students in full training, and, lastly, I have spoken specially about the opportunities offered to teachers outside the ordinary training curriculum who wish to qualify as recognised special teachers of physical exercises. These being the requirements, I should like to say a word or two, in finishing, about what are our practical desiderata in connection with this subject in the meantime, and how we can best secure these. I go back again to the note I struck earlier—that I think we want to emphasise quite strongly, in all the arrangements we make, the intimate relationship of physical training with the whole question of school and personal hygiene. It seems to me obvious that if the system is to work connectedly, smoothly, and efficiently towards the end we have in view, we must see, as far as possible, that from the very beginning the system is one consecutive, continuous whole. I am not speaking so much about the special details of any particular programme or curriculum of physical exercises. We have one which is pretty uniformly used all over the country at present. I am not speaking so much of that—although it is an essential element—as of the fact that, as far as we can manage, we ought to see that, from the time when this work begins—with the infant on his entry to school—to the time when it ends—in the turning out of the certificated teacher qualified by knowledge and training to teach this special subject—there should be unbroken systematic progress, step by step: no gaps, and no clashing or jarring at any stage, either when a new teacher is appointed or when a teacher is transferred.

How are we to manage that? We have started recently a sort of organisation which may, if it takes its proper place and is properly wrought, lead to a great deal of good in the way of co-ordination and systematising on lines such as I am speaking of—I mean the establishment of Provincial Committees, representing districts of Scotland, and charged with the very important duty of the training of teachers. It seems to me exceedingly important that these Provincial Committees charged with the turning out of teachers certificated for this work should know that the work, from its beginning, is proceeding upon a system which they understand as a Committee and as Managers, and are in sympathy with; and that the whole system should lead up to the Committees being able, at an important period of the professional training of their students, to utilise the student's time to the very utmost: not to waste his time upon doing school details which should have been done before, but to give him that broader outlook of the adult mind which ensures that he who is going to train others has a real grip and grasp of his subject, and to give him, further, such a power of teaching the subject as will make him really effective in the teaching of it.

These Provincial Committees being, as it were, the head educational bodies of divisions of Scotland, we have to look to the other existing educational authorities in the different parts of these divisions for co-operation in this matter. I think that the practical method of working is that the School Boards of the division which the Committee represents should do all they can to work in harmony with the Provincial Committee to see that this systematised and gradual progression is such as I desiderate. A good deal in that way has been done already. Glasgow, Aberdeen, and Edinburgh are moving, and the St Andrews Committee considered the matter the other day. The greatest help, to begin with, will come from the large Boards; and, fortunately, the Provincial Committees, being in the University towns, have large Boards as it were at their own doors. I hope that, by conference between the Committees and the representatives of these Boards, we may make at least a very hearty and hopeful beginning in this systematisation that I have been speaking of. Of course, the work cannot be carried out at all unless we get thoroughly competent instructors in physical training. We have not had many of these hitherto, but the subject is exciting interest, and I have no doubt that the supply of instructors will increase. We must, however, if we are to get at every school in the country, have thoroughly competent instructors distributed over the various areas. You see immediately what the difficulties are; but I think that, as a practical matter, we should concentrate meantime upon the junior student centres; and, so far as my personal advice with the Department can go, I shall advise very strongly that in connection with the work of all those schools recognised as junior student centres there shall be a thoroughly qualified instructor of the right stamp to take charge of the physical training.

But, even with these centres and these instructors, you still want some connecting and guiding hand to see that the system is carried out in the right spirit and in the right way throughout any one division. There I come to a point where the School Boards and the Provincial Committees may co-operate. The Committees are at present considering the appointment of two important officers—a lecturer upon school hygiene and an organising and supervising instructor in physical training. I am not prepared to say whether these offices can be combined; but, at any rate, I am very strong upon this point, that the two subjects must be essentially welded together—hygiene and physical training. If we must have two officers, the superior officer must be the one who looks at the whole matter from the foundation side of hygiene, and the supervising instructor must be a lieutenant to him. I am hopeful that within the next few years, by this hearty pulling together of all who are interested in the subject— professional and non-professional alike—we shall see a great rise in all that is done for the health and physical well-being of the children, and shall reap from that in later years a very, very rich harvest—the value of which, I believe, none of us can foresee just now.

` DISCUSSION.

Miss ROBERTS desired to know when it was proposed to begin training junior students to teach physical instruction?

Mr SCOUGAL said that the students would be trained in the art of teaching, and would practice the art of teaching, for at least six months during their three years' course. He should like to know if Miss Roberts, from her experience of the College, preferred that the junior students should have some practice in teaching the subject before they went to College?

Miss ROBERTS—No; I do not like them to have a smattering at one time and a smattering at another time. I think it is better for them not to teach at all until they are trained properly.

Captain FOSTER—The new system is just commencing, but the idea is that junior students at the age of fifteen shall be put under experts such as are being turned out here. During the first two years most of their time will be devoted to learning the actual movements, but in their third year, in combination with teaching of the laws of health and personal and school hygiene, they might, if they had made sufficient advancement, commence a certain amount of teaching under guidance, and in a manner that could do no harm in school. When they enter on their full course as students at the age of eighteen, then they should commence as soon as possible teaching the subject, but, again, under expert advice and supervision for the whole time. When the system is working fully, even children should know so much about the actual movements that when junior students begin their course at the age of fifteen they should make good progress, and be quite fit to commence teaching in their third year. Certainly between eighteen and twenty they should become, for school purposes, most efficient teachers of the subject. Of course, it will take years to work out the scheme. In many centres it will be difficult to get suitable tuition in physical training, but as time goes on the difficulties are bound to disappear. Some of the larger School Boards are now engaging the services of the best experts that money can procure in order that their junior students may be properly trained. The new Provincial Committees are also engaging the best possible experts for those in full student courses so as to continue their education in the subject between the ages of eighteen and twenty, until they become teachers in the Board schools. The Department are hopeful that, when the new system is in full working, by the time that the teacher gets to the Board school he or she ought to be quite able to take an active part in the physical training of his or her class as part of the ordinary school education. At the same time they hope that School Boards will continue the services of experts, and continue the education of teachers by means of courses of lectures, so as to keep up a high standard in physical education, and, if possible, to obtain a higher standard as time goes on. Of course, in the secondary schools you have quite different conditions. You are bound to have special teachers there for each subject; but in the Board schools I think it ought to be quite workable for the ordinary class teacher to undertake most of the physical exercises of the boys and girls.

Miss ROBERTS said she feared that they would never have efficient teachers of physical training in the Board schools until every teacher went through a definite and a sufficiently long course in learning to teach the subject. In the first place, they must be taught to use their voices; she believed that the inferior teaching in various schools in England was due to the teachers picking up words by attending classes, and not being trained to teach. The students must get definite teaching either at the junior stage or afterwards. One might be expert in physical training, but to impart it was a different thing. One of the great difficulties of the specialists was that they were asked to train people in twelve lessons. Even the proper use of the voice could not be taught in twelve lessons, and much of the actual benefit of the movements depended upon using the voice properly.

Captain FOSTER said that in five years they ought to turn out a fair teacher. If an expert were engaged for each Board school the cost would be enormous, and he doubted if the benefit, mentally and physically, would be so good as in the case of the ordinary class teacher doing the work. It was hardly fair to the experts that they should attempt to do the whole of the teaching. They were handicapped by not knowing the individualities of the children, and by the amount of work they endeavoured to overcome in a short time. They got a class of eighty for half an hour. At the end of that time a second class of seventy or eighty children was passed on to them. Half an hour later they had a third class of seventy or eighty, and their physical powers were not equal to this continual teaching. The result was that they never did their best work. In the Board schools the ordinary class teacher had opportunities for studying the individualities of his or her pupils, and that was important, since mental and physical education must go hand in hand. Having thought the matter out, it seemed to him that the undertaking of physical training by the ordinary class teacher was the only possible way of working the system and putting physical education on a higher footing in the Board schools.

Mr KIMBER, Dundee, said that in Dundee the children received graded exercises, leading them on to a certain stage of physical training. The junior students received a still further progressive course, which, however, only practically perfected the positions they had been taught in school. For the present, he did not himself see that it would be advisable to give the junior students any training in the art of teaching the subject. During the last six months of their course, however, they might be taught to give collectively the word of command. He did not think, however, that it would be advisable to have a snapshot here and a snapshot there. When the students came to College for a three years' course an endeavour was made to cultivate their voices as much as possible, and to give them such a good idea of teaching that they would practically go out as experts.

Mr STURROCK, Dundee, said that a good physical upbringing was the first essential of all education. If the conference should succeed in laying down certain great rules for the conduct of the work of physical training that would be known and obeyed by all instructors, they could then proceed with much greater certainty and hope of success.

Miss REID, Glasgow, said she found that the ordinary class teacher did very good work in connection with physical training in the schools. He took a great interest in the work and in school hygiene and the children under his charge; and she often found that the ordinary class teachers got better results than the expert. They had a better hold of the children, and got good work out of them. They insisted on open windows, and removed the children's superfluous clothing. She thought it would be found when the class teachers were better trained—through ordinary school courses and as junior students and teachers—that they would do just as good work as the experts, and perhaps better work.

The CHAIRMAN—Are you an expert?

Miss REID—Yes, but it is only the infant department that I have to do with.

Miss PALMER, Leith, said that although she also taught as an expert she very strongly agreed with Miss Reid that class teachers were much better fitted than experts to carry on the real training of the children. They were interested in "the new idea," as they called it, and she thought that with proper supervision they really did very much better work than the experts, because they knew the children so much better. They were with the children all day long. It was otherwise in secondary schools, where the pupils had different teachers for different subjects. She repeated that in the elementary schools the class teachers had it in their power to do better work than the experts, because the former knew the home conditions of the children, their physical state, and so forth.

The CHAIRMAN—You might explain what you mean by "proper supervision."

Miss PALMER—The appointment of a superintendent.

The CHAIRMAN—An expert?

Miss PALMER—Yes; some one to take charge of the schools and advise the School Board. I go round all the Leith schools. I have all the teaching in the schools under my charge. I train the junior students, too, and have evening lectures and practical work for the further training of teachers. Attendance at these evening classes is not compulsory, but a great many teachers have attended them and obtained certificates, and some of them are doing fairly good work in the schools.

Mr SCOUGAL—Do I gather that you have senior scholars in the schools as well as infants?

Miss PALMER—Yes, I have the entire supervision.

Mr SCOUGAL—Including the boys?

Miss PALMER—Yes.

Mr SCOUGAL—Have you classes for men teachers?

Miss PALMER—Yes, I supervise their teaching.

Mr SCOUGAL—You mentioned that you had the training of junior students. Would you give us the result of your experience on a point that is not quite clear? Would it, or would it not, be beneficial in your opinion to give the students at a later stage some training in the way of teaching the subject?

Miss PALMER—I have not had a great deal of experience yet. I only began with my junior students in October last; but I think that during the last six months or so they might begin teaching in an elementary way. It is difficult for me to judge, because I take it that they have not had any proper instruction in the schools before. They have to begin at the beginning.

Mr SCOUGAL—We must remember that at present physical training is at a transition stage. Four or five years hence it will be different. You will then get junior students who have had a three years' curriculum.

Miss RENDEL asked whether, in the event of the ordinary class teacher taking a mixed class, the men would teach girls physical training? If they did so, that would seem to her to be almost a retrograde step. In Dunfermline she had suggested that women should teach the girls and that men should teach the boys. She was told that that was not possible, because it would disorganise the arrangements of the school. The men were teaching the girls physical training in Dunfermline.

MR KIMBER said that in schools in Dundee the boys in the higher standards were taught by males and the girls by women.

MISS PALMER, in reply to the Chairman, said that in Leith the classes were mixed and she taught both boys and girls.

MISS GREY, Irvine, said that in the Academy she taught both boys and girls. It was a secondary or higher grade school, and the teachers were unable to teach physical instruction. In the elementary schools she supervised the teaching, which was given by the class teachers both to boys and girls.

THE CHAIRMAN—Is there any difficulty in controlling the boys?

MISS GREY—No, the boys and girls are always together.

THE CHAIRMAN asked Miss Rendel if she equally objected to ladies teaching boys?

MISS RENDEL—Well, boys require harder work and women cannot give it to them.

MISS GREY said that in her case the teaching of the boys was only temporary. There was no one to take the boys, and she just gave them a little exercise.

THE CHAIRMAN—By and bye there will be ladies for the girls?

MISS GREY—Yes.

Miss PALMER thought that girls should be taught by women and boys by men, especially in the older classes.

Miss RENDEL said that her remarks applied also to the teaching of hygiene. Girls and boys were taught together the laws of health. She thought it was a subject that it would be far better to teach separately.

Mr SMITH, H.M. Inspector of Schools for Fifeshire, said he was glad to hear that even the expert teachers bore out the view that Captain Foster and he had long held, that the teaching of physical exercises in the primary schools should be undertaken by the class teachers. He did not know that even Miss Roberts would dissent from that general proposition provided the ordinary class teacher had a sufficiently long training in the subject. If the principle he referred to were not acted on, the question appeared to him to admit of no solution, because it was only the class teacher who was in a position to give physical training on the lines they now desired. He wanted to emphasise the changed point of view. What they now aimed at, and what they wanted the teachers to keep before them, was the physical well-being of the individual child. It was not merely in physical training, but in all aspects of education, that such change of view as might be summed up in the phrase " well-being of the individual child " had come about within the last two or three years. It would be very interesting to go back over the whole history of the changes of view in regard to physical training and elementary education generally since the passing of the Education Act; but it

was quite clear that it was only within the last few years
that they had really gone back to this, the only true point
of view—that, what they had to consider both in regard
to the intellectual and physical as well as the moral side
was the individual child, and that nothing else mattered.
It was only the class teacher who was in school every day
who was in a position to know the needs and idiosyncrasies
of the individual child, and physical exercises, even if taught
on the best principles, would be of little use if only given at
such rare intervals as the visiting teacher could give them.
They were all agreed that to give these exercises their
proper effect they must be not only on a proper system, but
administered at regular and frequent intervals. One thing
more, do not let them start out with exaggerated views of
what the best course of physical exercises, taught by the
most expert young person that that College could produce,
would do for the individual. After all, the physical well-
being of the child depended on a great many other things
besides the particular system of physical exercises, and the
most important of these were things over which they had
extraordinarily little control. Let them remember that the
main object of physical exercises was a pretty humble one.
It was corrective—not so much the good they could do, as
the harm they could prevent. Still, that was a pretty
important object, but the statement of the fact might
perhaps suffice to bring them back to a more just perspective
of the place of these exercises in the school. He did not
undervalue the importance of physical training at all.

Captain Foster knew that for many years he had had a lively interest in the subject, and, if time permitted, he should be happy to tell what they were able to do in Glasgow to give effect to these ideas. But if they started out with an exaggerated idea of what they could do that could only result in disappointment, whereas if they started with a modest idea, the result would likely be very encouraging.

That brought him to another aspect of the question. The point they wished to attack at the present moment was the infant school. It was there, he thought, that the expert could do best service, especially if she were enlightened and brought to her work such breadth of knowledge and human interest as were displayed in Miss Rendel's lecture on the preceding day. With regard to the future, they were pretty safe in the hands of the Provincial Committees. They must rely upon the class teacher who came with a general certificate, but they always wanted to have within hail the expert, who could keep the class teacher up to the mark. There was quite a wide field for the expert, not only in advising the elementary teacher, but in actual teaching in the intermediate and secondary schools, where the subjects were specialised to such an extent that it was not possible for the class teacher to take the physical exercises. In towns the same teacher could be responsible for the physical training at the secondary school, and could also exercise supervision over the work of the elementary schools, as Miss Palmer did in Leith. Country schools occupied a different position, and in that connection he might state what was being done in Fifeshire. The County Committee intended to employ one or more lady experts, whom they proposed to hire out—if he might use such an expression—to those School Boards who wished to engage them. That was to say, the County Committee would engage the experts and be responsible for their salaries and travelling expenses. Country Boards would be invited to say how long they would like the services of the expert, and when the applications were received (some had come in already) a little route would be arranged here and there. For example, an expert would be stationed at Dunfermline for a few months, so that she might be able to overtake the supervision of the training in schools in the western corner of Fifeshire. He hoped that before the beginning of next session they should be able to invite applications from several experts for this kind of employment.

Miss ROBERTS, in reply to a question by Mr Smith as to what was being done during the two years of special training in physical instruction to maintain the general education of the students, said "Nothing whatever." The students of the Dunfermline College and other Physical Training Colleges in the British Isles had absolutely no time whatever even for general reading on their own account, and she did not see how they could ever turn out proficient teachers until they had a three years' course.

Mr SMITH—If you had a three years' course would you devote the extra year to general education?

Miss ROBERTS—I should devote a good part of the curriculum to general reading on lines where there would be some kind of supervision and guidance. I think it is a tremendous disadvantage—both from the point of view of the expert and the class teacher—that girls come at eighteen years of age to be trained and are turned out at twenty, when they are expected to train teachers. The age is too young; I should like to keep a girl until she was twenty-two, before she ever attempted her special training. Something should be done to get older students, and students of higher qualifications than those represented by the intermediate certificate. I may say that we have a great many students here with much higher certificates. Some of them were older before they entered, and had time for more extended education. I am sorry to say I am not yet a convert to the idea that the class teacher is the best for physical training even in the elementary schools. It is going back fifty years for a man to teach girls physical instruction. It is not going back for a woman to teach young boys.

Mr SMITH said that it seemed a good idea to extend the physical training course to three years, so as to maintain the general education of the students, but it was doubtful whether Scotland could afford such very highly qualified teachers as that. Regarding the teaching of boys and girls he agreed with what Miss Roberts and Miss Rendel said. The separation of the sexes should be matter of time-table arrangement. If the girls were separated from the boys two or three times a week for sewing, he did not see why that should not be done also in connection with physical exercises. He agreed also with what had been said regarding the undesirableness of teaching hygiene to mixed classes. The time to teach hygiene in school was between the ages of twelve and fourteen. The boys and girls were then in the supplementary course, and the classes ought to be divided according to sex.

Mr SCOUGAL asked Miss Roberts if she would accept a three years' course, or if, in the event of the course lasting for two years only, the students should begin at a later date, after their education had been more fully developed?

Miss ROBERTS said she thought that, upon the whole, better results would be obtained by having a full three years' course. Might she speak upon another point? She thought that Provincial Committees and School Boards in junior student centres did not realise what was fully recognised by those at that Conference—namely, that physical training was only part of hygiene. The expert was handicapped in not having authority to insist upon junior students and teachers wearing costume.

Captain FOSTER said that the system was only commencing. With time the difficulty to which Miss Roberts referred would disappear. They could not push the thing too fast. They had to educate people, and to educate School Boards and Managers of Schools. In many schools young pupils of ten, eleven, or twelve years of age now wore suitable costumes and suitable shoes when attending a gymnasium or taking their physical exercises in school.

Mr GEORGE SMITH, Aberdeen, said he was fully persuaded that if they were to tackle the future of physical education on the right lines they must at all cost get it into the hands of the class teacher. They must get the class teacher to realise that mental education was voluntary in character, and bound up indissolubly with the physical well-being of the child. If they put the ordinary intellectual instruction of the child into the hands of one person, and denied that person the physical training of the child, they were making the thing lop-sided. He thought that Mr Smith took too low a view of physical training when he said it was corrective. It was more, and the ordinary teacher must have in his or her mind a thorough conscious-ness of the fact that he or she was dealing with a growing organism—mental and physical. Unless the ordinary teacher had some knowledge of this fact that was scientifi-cally complete as far as it went, he or she was most certain to go wrong on certain points with reference to what Miss Ravenhill called "arrested development."

Miss RAVENHILL thought that in connection with the training of junior students the teaching of hygiene should begin rather earlier than the third year. The years from fourteen to sixteen were those in which habits were being most rapidly formed, and an intellectual acquaintance with the reasons for hygienic practice would be more impressive at such an important stage of life. At all events, it had been found so in the United States. She sympathised with Miss Roberts regarding the want of authority behind the expert teacher on the question of costume.

Mr SCOUGAL said that Captain Foster asked him to point out regarding the general question as to whether the expert or the class teacher should undertake physical training, that in his (Captain Foster's) experience school teachers had confessed to the great good it had done them to take an active part in the physical training of the children. They got more in touch with the children, and took a greater interest in them, and this re-acted upon the teaching of other subjects. Then, again, they got a definite improvement in an important matter—the management of their own voice. They acquired a better and a firmer kind of speech.

Miss RENDEL said she believed it was desirable and in many cases necessary that class teachers should teach their own class, but, before doing so, she thought they ought to have gained some knowledge of the intimate connection between physical and mental education. Unless they were very fully trained, would it not be better to allow an expert to have supervision of the school and to teach the girls in the supplementary course? She would be able to take them to more advanced and interesting work. It was very difficult for the ordinary teacher to interest the children in games and dancing.

Mr SCOUGAL—I am sure Mr Smith is quite with me in this matter. We have both spent a good deal of missionary effort in Glasgow in insisting that, at the supplementary course stage, specialisation very properly begins. I should agree with specialising on physical training being in the hands of the expert. It is a mere matter of arrangement; it is perfectly possible and desirable, and the next thing is to get the School Board to pay for it.

Miss ROBERTS said she did not see how the ordinary class teacher could learn to use her voice, learn to teach drill, games, dancing, hygiene, and the other branches of the subject that the expert was able to teach; and she did not think they would ever reach an ideal stage, or an enthusiastic stage, of physical training until they got an expert into each school.

THIRD DAY'S PROCEEDINGS.

"WHAT IS BEING DONE ELSEWHERE."

Miss ROBERTS Presiding.

Miss ROBERTS invited the visitors to give "short accounts of what is being done elsewhere."

Miss PALMER, Leith, said that she was superintendent and visiting instructor under the Leith School Board. She was allowed to make whatever arrangements she considered best. Having interested the class teachers in the subject, she started an evening class for teachers, at which there was quite a good attendance. She had about fifty pupil teachers on Saturday mornings. The arrangements for the training of junior students were not at all satisfactory. She hardly dare confess that she had them at four o'clock on two afternoons each week. The height, weight, and chest measurements of the children were taken annually. The Board were fitting up a handsome gymnasium as an annexe to one of the schools.

Miss RAVENHILL—Do you require that pupil teachers should invariably wear costumes?

Miss PALMER—Yes; I got them to do that when I took over the instruction myself. I divide the course into periods for theoretical instruction, practical work, and practising teaching. We have a course of twelve preliminary lessons and twelve advanced lessons. That is in addition to the help they are getting in the schools. The lessons last about an hour and a half each.

Miss GIBSON stated that she was superintendent of the Roman Catholic schools in Edinburgh and suburbs. There were nine schools. They were smaller than the Board schools, the number of children averaging 300. This enabled her to get round the schools once a week, and in some cases she saw the teacher every week. The accommodation in the schools was defective, and when the weather was bad they were very much hampered for space. Many of the teachers were nuns, and their dress was not very suitable for teaching, but she hoped soon to have more certificated teachers from the Training Colleges. During last winter she conducted evening classes for the teachers. Twenty-two lessons, each of an hour and a half, were given. She trained pupil teachers, giving them an hour each Monday night. They were in costume. At present no arrangements were made for junior students. She hoped to have them later on. There was some apparatus, but a gymnasium was going to be built soon at one of the schools. There was no necessity for having much apparatus at present, because the teachers were not able yet to give instruction in the use of it. The class teachers did not wear costume; only the pupil teachers did so.

Miss GREY, Irvine, said that she was appointed only temporarily for six months to superintend in the Board schools and take the teaching in the Academy. She had a teachers' class which she began almost at once in the evenings. At first it was arranged that they should have a course of twenty-five hours, but this had been extended to a sixty hours' course. They were having physiology and hygiene and much more theory than they would have been able to get otherwise. The instruction was divided into periods of an hour and a half, twice a week. Superintending the teaching in the four Board schools she was with each teacher half an hour every week; the teachers gave the other half-hour themselves. The number in the classes averaged from sixty to seventy, but an effort was being made to limit the number. There were only two or three pupil teachers, and they took the lessons along with the other teachers. Unless the course were extended, she did not consider it worth while to insist upon the wearing of tunics. The teachers were dressed as suitably as possible, without tight clothing. They always had shoes. She only taught the women teachers; she was asked to take the male teachers, but did not care to do so. There was a gymnastic apparatus at the Academy, and there was a probability of Swedish apparatus being introduced.

Miss THOMSON, Montrose, said that she taught in

the Academy and also in the elementary schools. She had not started a teachers' class yet, but such a class would be commenced in summer. She did not think she would insist upon the use of tunics, because she thought that some of the teachers would refuse to wear them. She apportioned two-thirds of her time to the Academy, and one-third to the three Board schools. She could only have about five classes in each of the Board schools. She did not teach the boys. Before she went, there was a drill instructor, and he continued to take the boys. She had a gymnasium at the Academy, fitted up with some Swedish apparatus. She had a gymnasium at one of the elementary schools, and at the other two schools she had to teach outside. She had done her best to get a class-room for another gymnasium, but the Board said that that was impossible. She had no apparatus in the Board schools, and did not press for it. She had half-hour classes of from thirty-six to forty children, and she would not get much done if exercises were given on one bar. The physical training was given only once a week. She hoped that later on it would be given oftener, and in that case she would endeavour to get more apparatus.

Miss ROBERTS asked if the children got another half-hour's training from the teachers?

Miss THOMSON—No, the teachers have not commenced to give instruction. I intend that they should make a beginning after the holidays.

Miss ROBERTS—Then there will be a second half-hour's training in each school?

Miss THOMSON—Yes, and perhaps ten minutes every day in the class-room, in addition to exercises once or twice a week in the gymnasium.

Miss DUDGEON, Edinburgh, stated that the teachers attended evening classes. She had four classes of teachers, to which she gave courses of thirty-six hours. About half or more of the teachers wore tunics, and those of them who did not have tunics had short skirts. All of them had shoes. Besides conducting the evening classes, she taught the girls in two schools. The children were supposed to get training from her on two half-hours each week. They were supposed to get half an hour's training from the other teachers, but she did not know whether they got it or not. She had eight or nine classes of girls, and the work was pretty heavy. She had no apparatus, and desired to get it, but it was difficult getting everything. She had no pupil teachers, but she trained the junior students. They just got a short half-hour—generally about twenty minutes —twice a week.

Miss ROBERTS—They have not begun to teach?

Miss DUDGEON—I give them very little of that. They are all quite new to the work. All wear shoes, and the majority of them have tunics.

Miss ROBERTS—How did they come to have the tunics?

Miss DUDGEON—I simply asked them to get them.

Miss RENDEL—If you get some teachers with tunics one week, you have others following their example the succeeding week.

Miss DUDGEON—Last year half the members of the class had tunics. This year the teachers came back for another course, and, with the exception of one or two, they have all got tunics. They also wear shoes very much more regularly.

Miss BROWN, Dundee, said that she superintended the working of twenty-three schools, including two academies, a school for cripples, and a school for deaf and dumb children. She began by teaching in the schools a great deal herself. For the first three months of her engagement she tried to work up physical training in five schools. Then gradually she turned her attention to other schools, but the result of this was that the teaching in the first five schools went back. Now she saw each teacher once in every four or six weeks for twenty minutes on each occasion. She found it practically impossible to get up teachers' classes for various reasons, but she was hopeful that she would be able to institute classes for teachers next winter. In one academy the teachers took the work, and she superintended. In the other academy half the pupils got physical training, also under her supervision. The other half had no physical work at all, owing to the overcrowded curriculum and want of space. She hoped that the Board would be induced to remedy this. The work in the school for deaf and dumb was very interesting. The head of the school was thoroughly keen on Swedish exercises. The children were doing very well. Physical training in the school for cripples was just beginning. The Fleming Gymnasium was designed for the

use of University students, but the authorities had been able
to get the use of it for students in full training, and she
had four hours a week training these students. There were
two classes, each having two hours a week, which included
the time available for teaching theory. She could not get
pupil teachers together during their normal school day. She
could only get them either early in the morning, or late at
night. She preferred to take them in the morning, and
they had two half hours a week—from nine o'clock to half
past nine. It was more a voluntary class than anything
else, but half the pupil teachers attended. She had them
in costumes and shoes. She was hopeful that they would go
on to the University and have the course extended. The
pupil teachers were not doing any teaching at all at present,
as she had to begin with them at the beginning. Her own
opinion was that pupil teachers should have some kind of
training in teaching. From her experience of teachers in
full training she thought that a two years' course was not
sufficiently long to instruct them in theory, practice, and
teaching. She thought that the junior students should have
a good deal of training in teaching.

Miss REID, Glasgow, said she had been asked to give
an account of what was being done by the teachers in
Glasgow. There were five working in Glasgow—three of
them almost wholly under the School Board, and two more
or less privately. Miss Watson had teaching in Park School
privately, and also worked in Helensburgh. Miss Smith
had a great deal of private work. She taught the students

in full training, and assisted with the teachers' classes. Miss Hunter and Miss Nasmyth worked together at the High School for girls. That was where she (the speaker) started work in 1900. She was there until 1905, when she was appointed to superintend the training in the infant departments under the Glasgow School Board. She had 77 schools under her charge, and it was difficult to get over these. It was not possible to visit them once a month, or even sometimes once in two months, because some of the schools required a great deal more attention than others. When she first went round the schools she had a great deal of opposition. Many of the infant mistresses had been teaching for twenty years, and they thought they knew more about the subject than any person visiting the schools. However, she did not think there was anyone now who was not interested, and who was not anxious to do her best. Many told her that physical exercises made the children much more alert and happier, and that it helped them in their other work. The children now received their drill without having a superabundance of clothing on. Last summer she gave a course of six lectures to between three hundred and four hundred teachers. They also had a little practical work to show how the work was conducted. During the winter before last, Miss Hunter started a class for teachers in the standard classes. She had seventy-five teachers altogether, who still had an ordinary gymnastic instructor over them. Last winter, a notice was sent to the teachers inviting the names of those who wished to attend a class, and between three hundred and four hundred names were sent in. A number were from surrounding country Boards, some coming a journey of an hour, or an hour and a half. Classes were held in the evening, and on Saturday morning. The teachers were very fresh and more enthusiastic on Saturday morning. After school work, they were tired in the evening—some of them also having drawing and painting classes to attend—and they were not really fit for physical exercises. Her hearers would be interested to know that she and her colleagues had managed to get the School Board to send material to the schools for use as handkerchiefs. In many of their schools the children were very poor, and such a thing as a handkerchief was unknown previously. Once or twice a day the children were asked to take out their handkerchiefs, and this was called "handkerchief drill." She had found that the desks were unsuitable in many cases, and the Board were putting dual desks into all the infant departments where the seats were without backs, and they were also going to alter some of the galleries. All the junior students were in costume when receiving their training. She did not think that the wearing of costume was compulsory; the students were simply told that it would be better if they had costumes. It was more difficult to get the members of the teachers' classes to wear costumes because some of them were older, but she had a number of them who were as old as any, who wore costumes.

Miss ROBERTS remarked that, under the London County Council, the teachers were obliged to wear costume, irrespective of age.

Miss REID—I think that will come. Some of them are very sensitive. I sympathise a little bit with them sometimes.

Captain FOSTER asked Miss Reid to state the time devoted to games and exercises in the infant departments?

Miss REID—When I first went round, the usual thing was to have half an hour once a week for drill, which was just moving their arms about. After that, we managed to get in a little drill, some time every day, irrespective of their half hour. Now, in most of the schools, we have drill between almost every lesson. That consists of just a few movements to waken the children up before they begin their next subject. The teachers find that it helps the work. It does not take up much time, and does not waste time. In most of the schools they have games; in one, twenty minutes or half an hour are set apart once a week for games. In several schools a game is introduced with the gymnastic lesson. Where they have no hall, they try to get in ten minutes' or fifteen minutes' drill every day at the desks, besides a few minutes between the lessons.

Miss BROWN—What is the longest period of work you give them when you take·them to a hall or playground?

Miss REID—Sometimes half an hour—that is including the time for taking the children to the hall and back again.

Miss SMITH, Glasgow, said that her work was rather mixed. Perhaps the most interesting part was her prison work. She had taught in Duke Street Prison for four and a half years now. She went there three times a week for periods of three quarters of an hour, and had from twenty-five to thirty women prisoners. On the whole, the work was quite satisfactory. It was rather difficult work, because she had a number of new prisoners at each lesson. She gave them very easy movements, and treated them just like children. On the whole, they did very well. She thought that the exercises did them a great deal of good, both morally and physically. She explained to them the physical benefits of the movements, and this interested them. She had also a class of between thirty and forty cripple children twice a week in conjunction with the School Board and the Queen Margaret College. They were not all cripples; some had skin diseases, some were epileptic, a great number were paralysed, and some were lame. A boy with one leg was very keen on going into the class, although she tried to persuade him that it was not much use. Some of them sat in their chairs and did the arm movements. She tried to introduce games. It was remarkable what the older cripple children could do. It sharpened the children, made them brighter mentally, and very much more attentive. She began the lesson by making them use their handker-chiefs (as most of them came from a poor class of people), and she strongly insisted upon personal cleanliness. She also taught the students who were undergoing their training under the Provincial Committee. There were, she thought, three hundred of them this year--about one hundred more than last year. She devoted two days a week to their training. She had them in the gymnasium at the University.

She was afraid it was rather a sorry gymnasium—one of the old-fashioned German kind, with only German apparatus. The period only extended to an hour a week, including dressing and undressing, which meant at least a quarter of an hour. Then, they were usually ten minutes late, because they never left the University at the time when they should really be with her. The great difficulty was that the students were overworked. They were taking their M.A. degree at the University at the same time as their teaching training, which was for three years. When they came to her they were thoroughly tired, and they simply dropped off by the score on account of brain fag and general ill-health. It was nonsense to expect them to do good physical work under these conditions. Miss Galloway, head of the Queen Margaret College, was doing her best to separate the training. If girls went in for the M.A. degree they must take it alone, and take their teaching training for one or two years afterwards, in place of trying to combine them. An hour or three-quarters of an hour a week was not nearly long enough for giving the teachers half the movements. They had no idea of using their voice so that it could be heard, and it was impossible to teach them the use of it in the time at her disposal. Then, she had the students at the Free Church Training College, as well as a class of children two hours a week belonging to the Training School. There was sometimes a mixed class of from sixty to eighty children, which was far too large. She made the boys take off their collars and also their coats—their chests being sometimes expanded with caps, books, and even on one occasion with a hot tea-cake. Many of the boys came with jerseys, which were suitable when their coats were taken off.

Dr ANNIE WATSON, Aberdeen, asked if the cripple children were medically inspected, or whether the physical training was left entirely in the hands of the teachers?

Miss SMITH said that the school was under medical inspection, the Medical Officer visiting it once a week or once a month.

Dr WATSON—Does the Medical Officer pass the children as suitable for the class?

Miss SMITH—The head teacher generally tells me if the child is unsuitable—if her heart is weak, or anything of that sort, so that I presume the Doctor has told her beforehand. She knows the complaints of every child, and is very careful.

Miss RAVENHILL—Do you discuss the condition of the children with the Doctor?

Miss SMITH—No; but I think it a very good suggestion that I should do so. I know the Doctor personally. On the whole, I do not think that any ill effects have arisen.

At the close of the discussion, Miss RAVENHILL lectured briefly on the advantages of using diagrams in the teaching of hygiene in schools. She also spoke of the necessity for teaching children to maintain a right posture, and condemned many of the desks used in school as being at variance with principles of health.

FOURTH DAY'S PROCEEDINGS.

"HINTS ON GIVING SHORT COURSES IN PHYSICAL TRAINING,"

By Miss E. ADAIR ROBERTS,

Principal of the Carnegie Dunfermline Trust College of Hygiene and Physical Training.

Dr ROSS Presiding.

Miss ROBERTS lectured on "Hints on giving Short Courses in Physical Training to County Council or Board School Teachers." She said—As a rule, the number of lessons in which an expert is expected to cover a complete, though elementary, course in physical training is inadequate. Twenty-five hour-lessons must be regarded as a minimum, and, indeed, a course of this length must only be regarded as a temporary measure, until a generation of teachers is turned out from the Colleges who have had Swedish gymnastics from the beginning of the junior student stage. The twenty-five lessons should be divided into a 30 minutes practical class--15 minutes lecture; 15 minutes commanding. As no person can understand the principles of scientific gymnastics except by personal experience in performing the exercises, it is perhaps a good fault to let the practical lesson encroach on the lecture occasionally. It should be borne in mind that a course of this kind is very likely a teacher's only chance of seeing movements, and of doing them with an opportunity of being corrected. Theoretical work can be read up at any time, if there is practical interest.

Short courses are usually mixed courses—*i.e.*, some teachers attending will have obtained previous instruction, while others will be quite new to the work; some will be infant mistresses, some standard mistresses, some youthful, and some past youth. For this reason, as well as for the technical one of giving the class a practical idea of "progression," the first lesson should be as simple as the first given to an infant school. The next three or four lessons should be one-step progressions on each other; after that progression should be sufficiently rapid to cover the whole work in an elementary school—say the 48 tables of the Handbook.

As a movement is given, the "expert" should point out that this is the balance exercise; this the shoulder blade, etc. The class should be asked where they feel the exercise, and to classify it by the feeling. When a difficult exercise is being led up to by an "introductory," this should receive comment.

It is so important that the teachers should visualise correct form in movements that I advocate personally showing almost every exercise before commanding it. With school classes the case is otherwise; the pupils are expected to memorise correct form in their muscles and nerves, and to imitate visually to a less extent, except in the infant departments.

Reference should frequently be made in the practical lesson to "progressions"—*i.e.*, show that in some previous lesson such and such a movement was given in "stride," but to-day in "close," etc., etc.

In teaching new positions and movements always anticipate the typical faults with a short warning. In this way an intelligent teacher will associate the right execution of a movement in herself, with a knowledge of what she is avoiding—*i.e.*, what she is likely to have to correct in children.

In free standing lessons it is very important to put in a lively march. It is often found that the untrained adult is slower to pick up the co-ordination of a fancy march than an untrained child. On this account the march must be analysed first, and then in the same lesson synthesized. An example of this is given in teaching polka march:—

1. Stamp three beats on the spot, with left leading; pause for 4th beat (left foot in crosswise position); stamp three more beats on spot, right leading, and pause 4th. Repeat *ad lib.* This exercise analyses for rhythm.

2. Repeat (1) advancing, for 4 complete movements.

3. Repeat (2) advancing on the toes.

4. Practice "and one"—*i.e.,* the jete off the right foot before the left step; and "and one" off the left foot before the right step.

5. Substitute 4 for each pause in 3—this is the polka march.

SUGGESTIONS FOR PURELY THEORETICAL INSTRUCTION IN TIME DEVOTED TO LECTURING.

Lectures should always be delivered in gymnastic costume. so that the "expert" can show any movement as she speaks about it. and gives it its technical name.

The expert should constantly revise her anatomy, physiology. and hygiene, apply and co-relate these subjects with her technical teaching. For instance, the discussion of lateral trunk movements naturally introduces question of corsets, while that of respiratory movements introduces ventilation. etc., etc.

Knowledge under the following heads should be considered essential to the theoretical work:—

(a) *Positions: Fundamental and Derived.*—Right execution and reason for it in each case; typical faults, and best words to use in correcting.

(b) *The Order of Movements.*—Reason for particular order of Swedish system: common sense reasons **for** occasionally not adhering to it. The classes **of** movement discussed separately in their order (definition, effects, execution, application, and progression).

(c) *Progression.*—Show the absolute need for progression in every class of movement, if gymnastics is to be considered part of education. Justify an increasing demand on pupil's power of attention and accuracy as age increases. Do not spend much time in purely mechanical discussions. Explain shortly, and ask for intelligent belief in, following methods of progression:—By decrease in base, by lengthening of lever, by changing the rhythm, or keeping it without counting.

(d) *Table-Making.*—Spend two or three lessons over this. Rule two table-blanks on blackboard. Ask class for movements in their order but otherwise at random. Go through the table thus formed to see if movements are of approximately the right difficulty, sufficiently different in style, and, lastly, with a view to finding out whether it is interesting. Make a second table, a one-step progression on the first, in the same way, changing the type of exercise as much as possible. An expert takes twenty minutes or half an hour to make up a good table for any class, even after years of experience. The ordinary class teacher may neither have time nor interest for table-making, and I therefore recommend their using "ready-made" tables till they gain experience.

(e) *Physiology of Exercise.*—Discuss the effect of exercise on all the systems of the body. Connect this discussion with Model Course Introduction—nutritive and educational effects, fatigue, etc. I believe this to be far more important and far more convincing than the particular physiological effects of each class of movement.

(f) *Model Course.*—Discuss as many points as possible from the preface and introduction of the Model Course. Show what a wide view these take of the subject, and how much is left to the teacher's intelligence and energy. Point out carefully any practical methods of your own, any words of command, any positions or movements in which you have taught the class differently from the Model Course regulations.

PRACTICE IN TEACHING.

The first half dozen or more lessons should be confined to "commanding," without the complication of standing up before the class, of trying to make corrections, or maintain discipline and exercise the memory.

The expert should make the class sit as for a lecture, and repeat commands after her, using a baton to indicate time as a musical conductor would do.

At first take short and simple commands to teach "pause," pitch, articulation, and force. Do these many times in class, and always give a few special ones to be practised.

Later, take commands where rhythm is peculiar ("leap on spot," etc.), or where time is difficult to keep (running). Later, take changes of time (march to run; polka to march, etc.). Later, tax the memory by commanding such a movement as point-stoop-stand. Sometimes ask individual members to command; at others, ask one line at a time, etc., etc.

In this way teachers learn to voice all the ordinary commands rightly from the beginning. If practice is vigorous enough at and between lessons, right commanding ought to come almost reflexly when the teacher stands up before her section for the first time. It is easier and more educational to learn correctly from the beginning than to attempt to form and alter bad habits. To test whether the class has grasped the idea of good form in movements, and of grappling with faulty positions, the expert should gather the teachers round her, do a movement with the typical faults, and ask an individual teacher to correct her. Go through every sort of movement in this way, as it is an easier matter to see faults than to use the right words in correcting.

DISCUSSION.

Miss PALMER asked Miss Roberts if she did not find that a great many class teachers were not able to do much practical work?

Miss ROBERTS said that she had had a few teachers of whom this might be said. The best thing to do was to give them a thorough knowledge of essentials.

Miss PALMER said that there were many teachers who were physically unfit for certain exercises. She had a medical examination, and, on the Doctor's authority, the teachers were forbidden to do various things.

Miss ROBERTS said she thought that all teachers ought to be medically certificated.

Captain FOSTER said that the Department advised the School Board that medical inspection should take place before a teachers' course was begun, so that none should take part who were physically unfit for the work.

Miss PALMER said that that would weed out a great many who might make excellent teachers, because it was not always those who did the best practical work who made the best teachers, but rather the reverse.

Miss SMITH thought that the instructors of teachers should work along with a Doctor, because many of the students were medically fit to begin with, but perhaps towards the end of the year they were anything but fit. She was often puzzled to know what to do. They had to go on with the work, and the instructor knew they were unfit, and the only thing she could do was to consult the Doctor. Perhaps this point was not sufficiently appreciated.

Captain FOSTER said that the medical examination of teachers had been going on, so far as he knew, since his appointment. In some cases School Boards had been careless, and had commenced teachers' courses before getting the sanction of the Department. Courses, therefore, might have been going on for a week or two before the Doctor had a chance of seeing any of the teachers. He might mention that many of these teachers' courses were held too soon. The School Board appointed a student, and within a week or two after she had entered on her duties, teaching in an academy and acting as visiting teacher in the elementary schools, a course was begun before the instructor had had time to know the class teachers. If the course could be postponed until about a year after the expert had been appointed, and after she had become acquainted with the teachers, and had had many talks together with them, it would be a good thing. There might even be a short course, so that they might become acquainted with each other. The regular course would then be a more effective one.

Miss ROBERTS was asked how long it took her elementary teachers to be able to distinguish between good and bad positions. In reply, she said that some teachers would never acquire ability to discriminate in this way. They were perfectly satisfied with certain positions, and would be so to the end of time. She thought their development had been such that they could not distinguish between good and bad positions by sight. She herself sometimes assumed typically erroneous positions, in order that the class might have an opportunity of detecting the defect, and explaining properly the correct position. It was not enough to be able to say—"Your hands are not right." They must be able to say in a word or two how the hands should be placed in order that the correct position might be assumed.

Miss PALMER asked Miss Roberts' view on the question of discipline in school?

Miss ROBERTS said that every lesson should have something interesting in it. If they made the children enjoy the lesson, it could not but be more effective.

Miss PALMER said that that was opposed to the class teachers' idea of discipline.

Miss ROBERTS—I know. They are afraid that if the children laugh, they will laugh too much. In the London schools, Swedish exercises often are a particularly dull affair, but that depends mainly on the teachers, as in secondary teaching.

Miss RENDEL said that she had made an experiment with reference to a disputed point raised at a previous sitting of the Conference. The question was discussed as to what age junior students should be taught to command, and it was suggested that the last six months only should be devoted to commanding; and that they should then begin their proper training as students in full training. She had experimented with her Health Course children, who had been with her, not only in that course, but in the schools for about two years, and had had a good deal of physical training work. Their ages varied from fourteen to seventeen. She found that when she took them out to command the class, the girls of fourteen had absolutely no difficulty in doing so. She supposed that they did it by imitation, but, at all events, the commands were given correctly. As soon as she got to the girls of sixteen and seventeen, they were like the junior students—they did not know how to look; they did not know how to command; they had not the correct intonation. That rather impressed her with the idea that it would be a good thing to begin with the younger students of fifteen; although they were not taught theory, let them command, because they would not have the same difficulties as they would have later. It never occurred to her younger girls that they could not command. The bigger girls, on the other hand, were self-conscious, and could not do it.

Dr ROSS said he should like to express, on behalf of the Carnegie Dunfermline Trustees, gratitude to the visitors for their attendance and for their contributions to the discussions.

On the motion of Miss LE COUTER, St Andrews University, the Trustees were thanked for the arrangements they had made in connection with the Conference.

Lightning Source UK Ltd.
Milton Keynes UK
UKHW021148061218
333419UK00013B/2043/P

9 780483 844551